ANOTHER DAY ON YOUR FOOT AND I WOULD HAVE DIED

Also published by Macmillan

ONE OF YOUR LEGS IS BOTH THE SAME
Poems by Adrian Henri, Terry Jones,
Colin McNaughton, Michael Rosen
and Kit Wright

WE COULDN'T PROVIDE FISH THUMBS
Poems by James Berry, Judith Nicholls,
Grace Nichols, Vernon Scannell,
Matthew Sweeney

Another Day on Your Foot and I Would Have Died

Poems by
John Agard
Wendy Cope
Roger McGough
Adrian Mitchell
Brian Patten

Illustrated by Colin McNaughton

MACMILLAN CHILDREN'S BOOKS

First published 1996 by
Macmillan Children's Books
This edition published 1997 by
Macmillan Children's Books
a division of Macmillan Publishers Ltd
25 Eccleston Place London SW1W 9NF
and Basingstoke

Associated companies throughout the world

ISBN 0 330 34048 4

7 9 8 6

A CIP catalogue record for this book is available from the British Library.

Typeset by Macmillan Children's Books
Printed by Mackays of Chatham PLC, Kent

Contents

The Missing Sock

I found my sock
beneath the bed.
'Where have you been
all week?' I said.

'Hiding away,'
the sock replied.
'Another day on your foot
and I would have died!'

Roger

Sensible-Bensible

Don't call me Silly Billy!
You know it's indefensible.
I wrap up when I'm chilly
And I'm sure two fives make ten.
So I'm not a silly-billy
I'm a sensible-bensible.
You're the silly-billy
I'm a sensible Ben.

Why *do* they say I'm silly?
It's quite incomprehensible
I cackle rather shrilly
When I imitate a hen,
And I ate a water-lily
Once – I can't remember when.
But I'm not a silly-billy,
I'm a sensible-bensible.
You're the silly-billy.
I'm a sensible Ben.

I don't believe it's silly
Or rude or reprehensible
To dance down Piccadilly
In my long johns, now and then.
My attire – warm, clean and frilly –
Is admired by other men.
You agree? Don't shally-shilly!
Must I spell it out again?
I AM NOT A SILLY-BILLY,
I'M A SENSIBLE-BENSIBLE.
Got that, Silly Billy?
Call me Sensible Ben.

My Rabbit

My rabbit
has funny habits.

When I say sit
he sits.

When he hears me call
he wags
his tail a bit.

When I throw a ball
he grabs it.

What a funny rabbit!

One day in the park
I swore I heard him bark.

John

You Can't Be That

I told them:
When I grow up
I'm not going to be a scientist
Or someone who reads the news on TV.
No, a million birds will fly through me.
I'M GOING TO BE A TREE!

They said,
You can't be that. No, you can't be that.

I told them:
When I grow up
I'm not going to be an airline pilot,
A dancer, a lawyer or an MC.
No, huge whales will swim in me.
I'M GOING TO BE AN OCEAN!

They said,
You can't be that. No, you can't be that.

I told them:
I'm not going to be a DJ,
A computer programmer, a musician or beautician.
No, streams will flow through me, I'll be the home of
  eagles;
I'll be full of nooks, crannies, valleys and fountains.
I'M GOING TO BE A RANGE OF MOUNTAINS!

They said,
You can't be that. No, you can't be that.

I asked them:
Just what do you think I am?
Just a child, they said,
And children always become
At least one of the things
We want them to be.

They do not understand me.
I'll be a stable if I want, smelling of fresh hay,
I'll be a lost glade in which unicorns still play.
They do not realize I can fulfil any ambition.
They do not realize among them
Walks a magician.

Brian

Tantrums

When my sister starts to frown
I'm always on my guard

Yesterday she threw a tantrum
But it missed me by a yard.

Roger

Grumbly Moon

'Turn that music down!'
Shouted the grumbly moon to
the rock 'n' roll stars.

Poetry Jump-up

Tell me if Ah seeing right
Take a look down de street

Words dancin
words dancin
till dey sweat
words like fishes
jumpin out a net
words wild and free
joinin de poetry revelry
words back to back
words belly to belly

dream! dance! Yes! lips! Bop!
me us up shine!
you cry! Jive!

Come on everybody
come and join de poetry band
dis is poetry carnival
dis is poetry bacchanal
when inspiration call
take yu pen in yu hand
if yu dont have a pen
take yu pencil in yu hand
if yu don't have a pencil
what the hell
so long as de feeling start to swell
just shout de poem out

Words jumpin off de page
tell me if Ah seein right
words like birds
jumpin out a cage
take a look down de street

19

words shakin dey waist
words shaking dey bum
words wit black skin
words wit white skin
words wit brown skin
words wit no skin at all
words huggin up words
an sayin I want to be a poem today
rhyme or no rhyme
I is a poem today
I mean to have a good time

Words feeling hot hot hot
big words feelin hot hot hot
lil words feelin hot hot hot
even sad words cant help
tappin dey toe
to de riddum of de poetry band

Dis is poetry carnival
dis is poetry bacchanal
so come on everybody
join de celebration
all yu need is plenty perspiration
an a little inspiration
plenty perspiration
an a little inspiration

John

Telling

One, two, three, four,
Telling Miss that Gary swore.
Five, six, seven, eight,
Now I haven't got a mate.

An Attempt At Unrhymed Verse

People tell you all the time,
Poems do not have to rhyme.
It's often better if they don't
And I'm determined this one won't.
                              Oh dear.

Never mind, I'll start again.
Busy, busy with my pen . . . cil.
I can do it if I try –
Easy, peasy, pudding and gherkins.

Writing verse is so much fun,
Cheering as the summer weather,
Makes you feel alert and bright,
'Specially when you get it more or less the
                    way you want it.

Wendy

My Dancing Granny

People speak a lot of rot,
Specially when they say
At a hundred and one my old Gran
Couldn't dance the night away.

A tea-dance or a hoe-down,
A fan-dance or the twist,
A tango or flamenco –
(She'll do them all if asked.)

You want to see her Charleston!
You want to see her romp,
She'll leap around the furniture,
Or simply stand and stomp.

She's no jumbo at the mambo,
She can shimmy with the best,
She can samba on till midnight
Without a moment's rest.

She'll bossa-nova over
To the youngest in the room,
And rumba till her lumba
Feels a twinge of gloom.

Then Gran'll do the can-can
And if the guests are still awake
She'll lead them in a conga line,
Or breakdance on a cake.

After a tot of sherry,
After wine with Sunday lunch,
After a nip of brandy,
She's the wildest of the bunch.

Fishing

Fishing all day long
and can't catch a thing.

What's wrong? What's wrong?
I ask the little worm
at the end of my hook.

The worm give me one look
and start to sing this song:

'Fish like to slip
in deep rain
Not take a dip
in frying pan.'

John

No Peas for the Wicked

No peas for the wicked
No carrots for the damned
No parsnips for the naughty
O Lord we pray

No sprouts for the shameless
No cabbage for the shady
No lettuce for the lecherous
No way, no way

No potatoes for the deviants
No radish for the riff-raff
No spinach for the spineless
     Lock them away

No beetroot for the boasters
No mange-tout for the mobsters
No corn-on-the-cob et cetera
    (Shall we call it a day?)

Roger

Keep Your Airplanes Away From Our Islands

the islands of Toronto
sleep upon the waters

small grass and friendly trees
are talking to the giant sky

a garter snake whispers across the path
the tyres of a bicycle whisper back

you can hear my brother singing to his boots
a squeaky song about the olden days
as the swing creaks him up to the sun

my mother plays the flute and her music makes
a fountain of birds fountain over the waters

you can hear so much on these lovely islands
which rose from the lake in an age of silence

you can hear the breathing of your best friend
you can hear the blood swimming around your veins

you can hear a slow and barefoot tread
which I believe is the sound of peace walking

peace upon the islands
peace upon the waters

as the islands of Toronto
sleep on the holy waters.

First Morning

I was there on that first morning of creation
when heaven and earth occupied one space
and no one had heard of the human race.

I was there on that first morning of creation
when a river rushed from the belly of an egg
and a mountain rose from a golden yolk.

I was there on that first morning of creation
when the waters parted like magic cloth
and the birds shook feathers at the first joke.

John

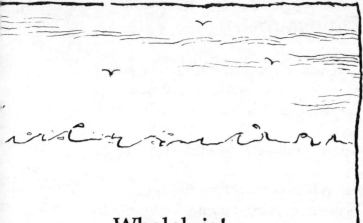

Whaleluja!

whales
are floating cathedrals
let us rejoice

cavorting mansions
of joy
let us give thanks

divine temples
of the deep
we praise thee

Whaleluja!

Roger

The Dinosaurs

They lived on our planet before there were people.
Forebears of our reptiles and fishes and birds,
They were not called dinosaurs then – they were
    nameless.
They lived on our planet before there were words.

Some were as tall as a four-storey building.
To keep themselves going, they needed to munch
The green things around them from dawn until twilight –
Their waking existence was just one long lunch.

Some preferred flesh. They would tear at their dinner
With terrible fingers and teeth sharp as knives.
Others grew horns, massive spikes, bony armour,
To ward off the carnivores, safeguard their lives.

They all disappeared and the world went on turning.
We humans evolved, with our language, our games,
Our hunger for knowledge. We found the lost creatures.
We dug up their bones and we gave them their names.

They stand in museums, grand skeletons, relics
Exhumed after millions of years in the ground.
And we are still learning. Who knows what strange
    monsters
Lie buried around us, and wait to be found?

The Pet Wig

Our teacher has a pet wig,
Nobody knows its name,
It clings to his baldy head
And looks extremely tame.

It's very calm and patient.
When dogs are on the prowl
It pretends it cannot hear the way
They clear their throats and growl.

It comes from a far-off land
(Or so we like to think),
A strange, endangered species
That's just about extinct.

After school he takes it off
And offers it some milk.
He strokes it extra gently
(Its fur is smooth as silk).

And in his lonely room at night
When he decides to retire,
He lays the wig quite carefully
On a blanket near the fire,

Where after a long day clinging
It rests content and purring.

The Cabbage is a Funny Veg

The cabbage is a funny veg.
All crisp, and green, and brainy.
I sometimes wear one on my head
When it's cold and rainy.

Roger

The Invisible Man's Invisible Dog

My invisible dog is not much fun.
I don't know if he's glad or glum.
I don't know if, when I pat his head,
I'm really patting his bum instead.

Rat It Up

C'mon everybody
Slap some grease on those paws
Get some yellow on your teeth
And, uh, sharpen up your claws

There's a whole lot of sausage
We're gonna swallow down
We're going to jump out the sewers
And rock this town

Cos we're ratting it up
Yes we're ratting it up
Well we're ratting it up
For a ratting good time tonight

Ain't got no compass
You don't need no map
Just follow your snout
Hey, watch out for that trap!

You can take out a poodle
You can beat up a cat
But if you can't lick a ferret
You ain't no kind of rat

Cos we're ratting it up
Yes we're ratting it up
Well we're ratting it up
For a ratting good time tonight

Now you can sneak in the henhouse
You can roll out the eggs
But if the farmer comes running
Bite his hairy legs

Check that cheese for poison
Before you eat
Or you'll wind up being served up
As ratburger meat

Cos we're ratting it up
Yes we're ratting it up
Well we're ratting it up
For a ratting good time tonight

This rat was born to rock
This rat was born to roll
I don't give a monkey's
Bout your pest control

So push off pussy-cat
Push off pup
We're the Rocking Rodents
And we're ratting it up

Yeah we're ratting it up
Yeah we're ratting it up
Well we're ratting it up
For a ratting good time tonight!

Adrian

Song

Eat thy bread with joy.
Ecclesiastes 9:7

I ate it with my supper,
I had some more in bed,
I breakfasted this morning
On Kilkenny brown bread.

Then I went out walking
Until my stomach said,
'You need a little salad
With Kilkenny brown bread.'

I'm not too good on rooftops
So I'll sing it here instead:
There's nothing as delicious
As Kilkenny brown bread.

If I get to Heaven
When I am gone and dead,
I hope the angels bring me
Some Kilkenny brown bread.

You can keep ambrosia
Unless it's thinly spread
On slices of miraculous
Kilkenny brown bread.

Fruit Jokes

The satsuma
Has no sense of humour
But a fig'll
Giggle

Adrian

Gust Becos I Cud Not Spel

Gust becos I cud not spel
It did not mean I was daft
When the boys in school red my riting
Some of them laffed.

But now I am the dictater
They have to rite like me
Utherwise they cannot pas
Ther GCSE

Some of the girls wer ok
But those who laffed a lot
Have al bean rownded up
And hav recintly bean shot

The teecher who corrected my speling
As not been shot at al
But four the last fifteen howers
As bean standing up against a wal

He has to stand ther until he can spel
Figgymisgrugifooniyn the rite way
I think he will stand ther forever
I just inventid it today

The Uncertainty of the Poet

I am a poet.
I am very fond of bananas.

I am bananas.
I am very fond of a poet.

I am a poet of bananas.
I am very fond,

A fond poet of 'I am, I am' –
Very bananas,

Fond of 'Am I bananas,
Am I?' – a very poet.

Bananas of a poet!
Am I fond? Am I very?

Poet bananas! I am.
I am fond of a 'very'.

I am of very fond bananas.
Am I a poet?

No Hickory No Dickory No Dock

Wasn't me
Wasn't me
said the little mouse
I didn't run up no clock

You could hickory me
You could dickory me
or lock me in a dock

I still say
I didn't run up no clock

Was me who ran under your bed
Was me who bit into your bread
Was me who nibbled your cheese

But please please,
I didn't run up no clock
no hickory
no dickory
no dock.

John

Checking Out Me History

Dem tell me
Dem tell me
Wha dem want fo tell me

Bandage up me eye with me own history
Blind me to me own identity

Dem tell me bout 1066 and all dat
Dem tell me bout Dick Whittington and he cat
But Toussaint L'Ouverture
no dem never tell me bout dat

Toussaint[1]
a slave
with vision
lick back
Napoleon
battalion
and first Black

Republic born
Toussaint de thorn
to de French
Toussaint de beacon
of de Haitian Revolution

Dem tell me bout de man who discover de balloon
and de cow who jump over de moon

Dem tell me bout de dish run away with de spoon
but dem never tell me bout Nanny de maroon[2]

Nanny
see-far woman
of mountain dream
fire-woman struggle
hopeful stream
to freedom river

Dem tell me bout Lord Nelson and Waterloo
but dem never tell me bout Shaka de great Zulu
Dem tell me bout Columbus and 1492
but what happen to de Caribs[3] and de Arawaks too

Dem tell me bout Florence Nightingale and she lamp
and how Robin Hood used to camp

Dem tell me bout old King Cole was a merry ole soul
but dem never tell me bout Mary Seacole[4]

From Jamaica
she travel far
to the Crimean War
she volunteer to go
and even when de British said no
she still brave the Russian snow
a healing star
among the wounded
a yellow sunrise
to the dying

Dem tell me
Dem tell me wha dem want fo tell me
By now I checking out me own history
I carving out me identity.

Notes:
1 Toussaint L'Ouverture. Rarely mentioned in school history
books. A slave who led an army that defeated forces sent by
Napoleon.
2 Nanny. A national heroine of Jamaica. She led runaway slaves
to establish a free colony in the hills of Jamaica.
3 Caribs. Amerindian tribe from whom the Caribbean got its
name.
4 Mary Seacole. The Jamaican nurse who put her skills to use in
the Crimean War (1853-6) but who did not receive the acclaim
that Florence Nightingale did.

A Good Poem

I like a good poem.
One with lots of fighting
in it. Blood, and the
clanging of armour. Poems

against Scotland are good,
and poems that defeat
the French with crossbows.
I don't like poems that

aren't about anything.
Sonnets are wet and
a waste of time.
Also poems that don't

know how to rhyme.
If I was a poem
I'd play football and
get picked for England.

Roger

School Dinners

Lumpy custard and liver – ugh!
I hate school dinners and I'll tell you why.
There's dog food with peas in, there's Secret Stew,
And a cheese and bacon thing we call Sick Pie.

Adrian

Nothingmas Day

No it wasn't.

It was Nothingmas Day and all the children in Notown were
not tingling with excitement as they lay unawake in their
heaps.
D
  o
    w
      n
        s
          t
            a
              r
                s their parents were busily not placing the
last crackermugs, glimmerslips and sweetlumps on the
Nothingmas Tree.

Hey! But what was that invisible trail of chummy sparks or
vaulting stars across the sky?
  Father Nothingmas – drawn by 18 or 21 rainmaidens!
  Father Nothingmas – his sackbut bulging with air!
  Father Nothingmas – was not on his way!
(From the streets of the snowless town came the quiet of
unsung carols and the merry silence of the steeple bell.)

Next morning the children did not fountain out of bed with
cries of WHOOPERATION! They picked up their
Nothingmas Stockings and with traditional quiperamas such
as: 'Look what I haven't got! It's just what I didn't want!'
pulled their stockings on their ordinary legs.

For breakfast they ate – breakfast.

Afterwoods they all avoided the Nothingmas Tree, where Daddy, his face failing to beam like a leaky torch, was not distributing gemgames, sodaguns, golly-trolleys, jars of humdrums and packets of slubberated croakers.

Off, off, off went the children to school, soaking each other with no howls of 'Merry Nothingmas and a Happy No Year!', and not pulping each other with no-balls.

At school Miss Whatnot taught them to write No Thank You Letters.

Home they burrowed for Nothingmas Dinner.
The table was not groaning under all manner of

NO TURKEY
NO SPICED HAM
NO SPROUTS
NO CRANBERRY JELLYSAUCE
NO NOT NOWT

There was not one shoot of glee as the Nothingmas
Pudding, unlit, was not brought in. Mince pies were not
available, nor was there any demand for them.

Then, as another Nothingmas clobbered to a close, they all
haggled off to bed where they slept happily never after.

and that is not the end of the story . . .

Adrian

Playing Football With the Dog

Arthur Sneer played football with his dog.
How cruel can you get?

Kate

who became obsessed with a puzzle and went mad.

No-one could call Kate depraved.
In fact, she was quite well-behaved.
She didn't want to spend her time
Engaged in mischief, or in crime,
Or gazing at the TV tube
But fiddling with her Rubik cube.

Every day when she awoke,
Before she washed or dressed or spoke,
She'd pick it up and give a twist
And, once begun, she must persist
Through breakfast (though the cube got sticky)
And all through school – but that was tricky.

Teachers used to go berserk:
'Give me that cube and do your work!'

Kate thought their attitude grotesque.
She kept a spare cube in her desk.

Turn and twist and twist and turn –
The puzzle was her one concern.
However much she might revolve it
It seemed that she would never solve it.
When she got the green side right
The reds were all mixed up with white.
When the reds were on one face
The greens were once more out of place.
Like the spider seen by Bruce,
Kate tried and tried again – no use:
Yellow was still mixed up with blue
And there were three more sides to do.
Other children called it quits
And took their Rubik cubes to bits.
Kate kept going – she had guts,
Though was slowly going nuts.
Soon she could not sleep or eat
But she would not admit defeat.
She grew pale and weak and puny.
People said, 'That Kate's a loony!'

Men in white coats came one day
And took our heroine away.
Her parents sobbed, 'It's very sad.
We knew that cube would drive her mad.'

Wendy

The Pet Habit

I'm fed up people telling me
I've got a nasty habit.
But I have. It's true. I do.

I keep it in a box full of dirty straw.
I feed it nose-pickings and belches,
Bits of spit and bum-scratches.
It's a nasty little habit.
When people ask 'What's in that box?'
I say, 'It's my pet habit.'
'Don't you mean pet rabbit?' they ask.
'No,' I say, and show them.
'That's a nasty little habit,' they say.

Catapillow

A catapillow
is a useful pet

To keep
upon your bed

Each night you simply
fluff him up

Then rest
your weary head.

Roger

I've Taken To My Bed

I've taken to my bed
(And my bed has taken to me)
We're getting married in the spring
How happy we shall be

We'll raise lots of little bunks
A sleeping-bag or two
Take my advice: find a bed that's nice
Lie down and say: 'I love you.'

Roger

First Day at School

A millionbillionwillion miles from home
Waiting for the bell to go. (To go where?)
Why are they all so big, other children?
So noisy? So much at home they
must have been born in uniform.
Lived all their lives in playgrounds.
Spent the years inventing games
that don't let me in. Games
that are rough, that swallow you up.

And the railings.
All around, the railings.
Are they to keep out wolves and monsters?
Things that carry off and eat children?
Things you don't take sweets from?
Perhaps they're to stop us getting out.
Running away from the lessins. Lessin.
What does a lessin look like?
Sounds small and slimy.
They keep them in glassrooms.
Whole rooms made out of glass. Imagine.

I wish I could remember my name.
Mummy said it would come in useful.
Like wellies. When there's puddles.
Yellowwellies. I wish she was here.
I think my name is sewn on somewhere.
Perhaps the teacher will read it for me.
Tea-cher. The one who makes the tea.

Roger

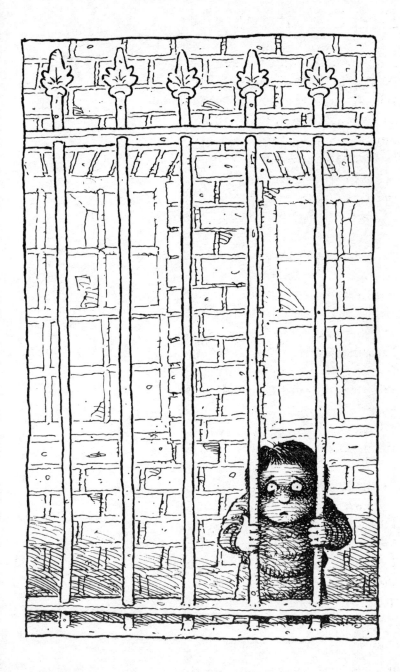

Not a Very Cheerful Song, I'm Afraid

There was a gloomy lady,
With a gloomy duck and a gloomy drake,
And they all three wandered gloomily,
Beside a gloomy lake,
On a gloomy, gloomy, gloomy, gloomy, gloomy,
  gloomy day.

Now underneath that gloomy lake
The gloomy lady's gone.
But the gloomy duck and the gloomy drake
Swim on and on and on,
On a gloomy, gloomy, gloomy, gloomy, gloomy,
  gloomy day.

Adrian

The Sound Collector

A stranger called this morning
Dressed all in black and grey
Put every sound into a bag
And carried them away

The whistling of the kettle
The turning of the lock
The purring of the kitten
The ticking of the clock

The popping of the toaster
The crunching of the flakes
When you spread the marmalade
The scraping noise it makes

The hissing of the frying-pan
The ticking of the grill
The bubbling of the bathtub
As it starts to fill

The drumming of the raindrops
On the window-pane
When you do the washing-up
The gurgle of the drain

The crying of the baby
The squeaking of the chair
The swishing of the curtain
The creaking of the stair

A stranger called this morning
He didn't leave his name
Left us only silence
Life will never be the same.

Roger

Kindness to Animals

If I went vegetarian
And didn't eat lambs for dinner,
I think I'd be a better person
And also thinner.

But the lamb is not endangered
And at least I can truthfully say
I have never, ever eaten a barn owl,
So perhaps I am OK.

Allivator

at the top.
then eat you
his back
ride upon
let you
he will
in a shop
see one
if you
allivator
Beware the

Roger

Spell to Banish a Pimple

Get back pimple
get back to where you belong

Get back to never-never land
and I hope you stay there long

Get back pimple
get back to where you belong

How dare you take up residence
in the middle of my face

I never offered you a place
beside my dimple

Get back pimple
get back to where you belong

Get packing pimple
I banish you to outer space

If only life was that simple

Simple Pimple Spells

Secret

Tell me your secret.
I promise not to tell.
I'll guard it safely at the bottom of a well.

Tell me your secret.
Tell me, tell me, please.
I won't breathe a word, not even to the bees.

Tell me your secret.
It will be a pebble in my mouth.
Not even the sea can make me spit it out.

John

Huff

I am in a tremendous huff –
Really, really bad.
It isn't any ordinary huff –
It's one of the best I've had.

I plan to keep it up for a month
Or maybe for a year
And you needn't think you can make me smile
Or talk to you. No fear.

I can do without you and her and them –
Too late to make amends.
I'll think deep thoughts on my own for a while,
Then find some better friends.

And they'll be wise and kind and good
And bright enough to see
That they should behave with proper respect
Towards somebody like me.

I do like being in a huff –
Cold fury is so heady.
I've been like this for half an hour
And it's cheered me up already.

Perhaps I'll give them another chance,
Now I'm feeling stronger
But they'd better watch out – my next big huff
Could last much, much, much longer.

Nobody Rides The Unicorn

His coat is like snowflakes
Woven with silk.
When he goes galloping
He flows like milk.

His life is all gentle
And his heart is bold.
His single horn is magical
Barley sugar gold.

Nobody rides the Unicorn
As he grazes under a secret sun.
His understanding is so great
That he forgives us, every one.

Nobody rides the Unicorn,
His mind is peaceful as the grass.
He is the loveliest one of all
And he sleeps behind the waterfall.

P's and Q's

I puite often confuse

My quees and my poos.

Roger

Burying the Dog in the Garden

When we buried
the dog in
the garden on
the grave we put
a cross and
the tall man
next door was
cross.
'Animals have no
souls,' he said.

'They must have animal
souls,' we said. 'No,'
he said and
shook his head.
'Do you need a
soul to go
to Heaven?' we
asked. He nodded
his head. 'Yes,'
he said.
'That means my
hamster's not
in Heaven,' said
Kevin. 'Nor is
my dog,' I said.
'My cat could sneak
in anywhere,' said
Clare. And we thought
what a strange place Heaven
must be with
nothing to stroke
for eternity.
We were all
seven.
We decided we
did not want to
go to Heaven.
For that the
tall man next
door is to blame.

Who Is de Girl?

who is de girl dat kick de ball
then jump for it over de wall

sallyann is a girl so full-o zest
sallyann is a girl dat just can't rest

who is de girl dat pull de hair
of de bully and make him scare

sallyann is a girl so full-o zest
sallyann is a girl dat just can't rest

who is de girl dat bruise she knee
when she fall from de mango tree

sallyann is a girl so full-o zest
sallyann is a girl dat just can't rest

who is de girl dat set de pace
when boys and girls dem start to race

sallyann is a girl so full-o zest
sallyann is a girl dat just can't rest

John

Dear Mum,

while you were out
a cup went and broke itself,
a crack appeared in the blue vase
your great-great grandad
brought back from Mr Ming in China.
Somehow, without me even turning on the tap,
the sink mysteriously overflowed.
A strange jam-stain,
about the size of a boy's hand,
appeared on the kitchen wall.
I don't think we will ever discover
exactly how the cat
managed to turn on the washing-machine
(specially from the inside),
or how Sis's pet rabbit went and mistook
the waste-disposal unit for a burrow.
I can tell you I was scared when,
as if by magic,
a series of muddy footprints
appeared on the new white carpet.
I was being good
(honest)
but I think the house is haunted so,
knowing you're going to have a fit,
I've gone over to Gran's for a bit.

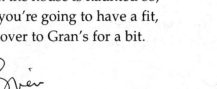

So-So Joe

So-So Joe
de so-so man
wore a so-so suit
with a so-so shoe.
So-So Joe
de so-so man
lived in a so-so house
with a so-so view.
And when you asked
So-So Joe
de so-so man
How do you do?
So-So Joe
de so-so man
would say to you:

> Just so-so
> Nothing new.

John

Having My Ears Boxed

I am waiting in the corridor
To have my ears boxed.
I am nervous, for Mr O'Hanlon
Is a beast of his word.

For the last twenty minutes
I have let my imagination
Run away with itself.
But I am too scared to follow.

Will he use that Swiss Army knife
To slice through cleanly? Bite them off?
Tear carefully along perforated lines?
Tug sharply like loose Elastoplasts?

Acknowledging the crowd's roar
Will he hold my head aloft
As if it were the FA Cup
And pull the handles? Aagghhrr . . .

And then the box. Cardboard?
Old cigar-box possibly? Or a pair?
Separate coffins of polished pine.
Left and Right. 'Gone to a better place.'

Impatient now, I want to get it
Over with. Roll on four o'clock.
When, hands over where-my-ears-used-to-be
I run the gauntlet of jeering kids.

At six, mother arrives home weary
After a hard day at the breadcrumb factory.
I give her the box. She opens it
And screams something. I say:

'Pardon?'

Roger

Guess What Dad Does

When I went to junior school
My friends asked what Dad did.
I did not dare to tell them,
So I had to ad lib.

My father's not a fireman.
He's not a bus conductor.
He's not a stuntman in the films
Or a PE instructor.

Yes he is quite rich,
And no, he's not a banker.
He doesn't own a goldmine
Or an oil tanker.

I help him with his job,
And stay up late at night.
Dad works in the shadows
And does not like the light.

I like his job best of all,
And I get quite excited
When we enter people's homes
Totally uninvited.

Kenneth

*who was too fond
of bubble-gum and
met an untimely end.*

The chief defect of Kenneth Plumb
Was chewing too much bubble-gum.
He chewed away with all his might,
Morning, evening, noon and night,
Even (oh, it makes you weep)
Blowing bubbles in his sleep.
He simply couldn't get enough –
His face was covered with the stuff.
As for his teeth – oh, what a sight!
It was a wonder he could bite.
His loving mother and his dad
Both remonstrated with the lad.
Ken repaid them for their trouble
By blowing yet another bubble.

'Twas no joke. It isn't funny
Spending all your pocket money
On the day's supply of gum –
Sometimes Kenny felt quite glum.
As he grew, so did his need –
There seemed no limit to his greed:
At ten he often put away
Ninety-seven packs a day.

Then at last he went too far –
Sitting in his father's car,
Stuffing gum without a pause,
Found that he had jammed his jaws.
He nudged his dad and pointed to
The mouthful that he couldn't chew.
'Well, spit it out if you can't chew it!'
Ken shook his head. He couldn't do it.
Before long he began to groan –
The gum was solid as a stone.
Dad took him to a builder's yard;
They couldn't help. It was too hard.
They called a doctor and he said,
'This silly boy will soon be dead.
His mouth's so full of bubble-gum,
No nourishment can reach his tum.'

Remember Ken and please do not
Go buying too much you-know-what.

Washing-Up Day

Clothes in a tub
rub rub rub.
Clothes in a tub
rub rub rub.
Hand in soapy water-o
Hand in soapy water-o

Clothes in a tub
rub-um squeeze-um.
Clothes in a tub
rub-um wring-um.
Hand in soapy water-o
Hand in soapy water-o

Clothes in a tub
come nice and clean,
but I saving up
me money
for washing-machine

John

In Good Hands

Wherever night falls

The earth is always

There to catch it.

Roger

Yes

A smile says: Yes.
A heart says: Blood.
When the rain says: Drink
The earth says: Mud.

The kangaroo says: Trampoline.
Giraffes say: Tree.
A bus says: Us,
While a car says: Me.

Lemon trees say: Lemons.
A jug says: Lemonade.
The villain says: You're wonderful.
The hero: I'm afraid.

The forest says: Hide and Seek.
The grass says: Green and Grow.
The railway says: Maybe.
The prison says: No.

The millionaire says: Take.
The beggar says: Give.
The soldier cries: Mother!
The baby sings: Live.

The river says: Come with me.
The moon says: Bless.
The stars say: Enjoy the Light.
The sun says: Yes.

Adrian

Uncle Ben from Number One

Uncle Ben was not a hen
But when he laid an egg
He did it quite professionally
By lifting up a leg.

He studied it and prodded it
And said 'I'm mystified.'
And then he took it to the kitchen
Where he had it, fried.

INDEX OF AUTHORS AND FIRST LINES

JOHN AGARD

John Agard was born in Guyana, a South American mainland country that's part of the Caribbean.

He writes for the little people, the big people and the in-between people. When asked 'Did you always want to be a poet?' he has to say 'No.'

At fourteen he acted as Captain Hook in *Peter Pan* and loved taking part in school plays, so he thought he might be an actor. At St. Stanislaus College, a Roman Catholic Secondary School, he served mass as an altar boy and thought he might be a priest. But he also enjoyed pretending he was a cricket commentator, just like the man in the radio, and in his pretend commentaries he'd throw in words like 'spectacular boundary' and 'marvellous delivery', not realising he himself was becoming hooked on words.

Looking back, there's a bit of the actor, the priest *and* the cricket commentator in the poet, and each is entitled to a glass of wine, though he prefers a drop of Guinness.

Since 1977, he has been living in the UK, where he has performed his poetry widely in schools, festivals and on radio and TV.

His collections of poetry include *I Din Do Nuttin, Say it Again Granny, Laughter is an Egg*, and a teenage collection *Get Back Pimple*.

WENDY COPE

When Wendy Cope was a little girl she liked reading, writing stories, and playing with her dolls. She did not like going for walks, going to church, or listening to grown-ups talking about their gardens.

When she grew up she became a primary school teacher in London. She still liked reading but she had forgotten all about writing, until she began encouraging her class to write poems, and found she could do it too.

Now she has given up teaching and lives in Winchester. She likes reading, writing (sometimes), going for walks, and services in Winchester Cathedral. She is very interested in gardening.

ROGER McGOUGH

Born in Liverpool, Roger McGough wrote his first poem at the age of seventeen.

As well as teaching, then singing on *Top of the Pops*, he has been writing and performing poems for aeons.

He has the largest collection of missing socks in London.

ADRIAN MITCHELL

Adrian Mitchell was born in London and educated by wolves. His first play – *The Animals' Brains Trust* – was performed when he was nine. Since then he has written poetry, plays, TV plays and stories for adults and children.

His books for children include the *Our Mammoth* and *The Baron* stories, *The Orchard Book of Poems, All My Own Stuff* and *The Thirteen Secrets of Poetry.*

His golden retriever, Ella Mitchell, is a distinguished archaeologist and the mother of ten puppies; six golden and four black. He also has a black cat with white socks called Billie and a nervous tabby called Gnasher.

BRIAN PATTEN

Brian Patten writes poems for adults as well as for children, and hopes those who read his children's poetry will one day read his adult poems as well.

He has slept under a blanket in the desert among ancient ruins, and has travelled through some of the highest mountains in the world. He once visited the remote volcanic islands of the Galapagos – a thousand kilometres west of the Ecuadorian coast – where he saw huge iguanas, which resembled prehistoric dinosaurs. He loves swimming in the sea and once saved the life of an octopus that had become trapped in a tiny underwater cave by a piece of plastic. His books of poetry include *Gargling With Jelly* and *Thawing Frozen Frogs*. He has a cat called Wiz and likes gardening.

COLIN McNAUGHTON

I was born in the north-east of England at an extraordinarily early age. In fact, legend has it that I was born at the age of nought. I was always treated as a special child. Some point out this was because by the age of two I was six feet tall and could speak sixteen languages backwards. (Unfortunately I couldn't speak any of them forwards.)

My early dreams of playing centre forward for Newcastle United were cruelly dashed when, at the age of six, I was turned down by the then manager Mr Joe 'bring 'im down!' Plankton. He said my footballing skills were wonderful, but because I was still talking backwards at this time, I failed the oral test. My attempts at common football phrases came out as '.Saint ,game old funny a It's' and '.halves two of game a Football's'.

Brushing disappointment aside I ran away to sea and joined a pirate ship called the *Golden Behind* as a cabin boy. However, Captain Abdul the Skinhead and his crew did not sail the Seven Seas, they just sort of hung around the mouth of the River Tyne.

We did steal tons and tons of stuff, though: the Captain called it 'Black Gold'; I called it 'coal'.

At the age of seven I travelled to London and got a job as Prime Minister, but was sacked for extending the school summer holidays to fifty-one weeks plus one for Christmas. Luckily, as I was removing my belongings from 10 Downing Street, a policeman stopped me and said 'Colin, I hear there's a job going at Buckingham Palace. Why don't you apply for it?'

I started the next morning as Prince Phillip, the Duke of Edinburgh. After opening several sewage disposal works it was pointed out one day by a small boy that I looked nothing like Prince Phillip (this was true). Once again I was unemployed. It was then I decided it was about time I had a proper education so, at the age of nine and a bit, purchased an armadillo and enrolled in the Vinny Jones Academy of Verse and Drawing. The rest, as they say, is 'poetry'.

Acknowledgements

The publishers would like to thank the following for permission
to reprint the selections in this book:

Caroline Sheldon Literary Agency for 'Washing Up Day', 'So-So Joe' and 'No Hickory No
Dickory No Dock' from No Hickory No Dickory No Dock © John Agard 1991 first published by
Viking; 'Who Is De Girl?' from Strawberry Drums published by Macdonald Children's Books
1989; 'Fishing', 'My Rabbit' from I Din Do Nuttin published by Bodley Head 1983; 'First
Morning' from Laughter is An Egg published by Viking 1990; 'Spell To Banish A Pimple' from
Life Doesn't Scare Me At All published by Heinemann 1989; 'Checking Out Me History' from
New Angles published by Oxford University Press 1987; 'Secret' from Get Back Pimple published
by Viking 1995; 'Poetry Jump Up' from You'll Love This Stuff published by
Cambridge University Press 1986.

Faber and Faber Ltd for 'Telling' from Twiddling Your Thumbs © Wendy Cope 1988 and for 'The
Uncertainty Of The Poet' and 'Kindness To Animals' from Serious Concerns © Wendy Cope
1992; 'Kate', 'Kenneth', 'An Attempt at Unrhymed Verse', 'Huff', 'Sensible-Bensible', 'Kilkenny
Brown Bread', 'Dinosaurs' © Wendy Cope 1995.

Peters Fraser & Dunlop for 'I've Taken To My Bed', 'Missing Sock', 'Tantrums','Sound
Collector' from Pillow Talk © Roger McGough 1990 first published by Viking; 'The Cabbage Is A
Funny Veg', 'Whale Poems' from Sky In The Pie © Roger McGough 1983 first published by
Kestrel Books; 'Catapillow' and 'Allivator' from The Imaginary Menagerie © Roger
McGough1988 first published by Viking Kestrel; 'In Good Hands' and 'P's & Q's' from Nailing
The Shadow © Roger McGough 1987 first published by Viking Kestrel; 'Having My Ears Boxed'
from Defying Gravity © Roger McGough 1991, 1992 first published by Viking; 'First Day At
School' and 'A Good Poem' from In The Glassroom © Roger McGough 1976 first published by
Jonathan Cape, 'No Peas For the Wicked' from Lucky © Roger McGough 1993 first
published by Viking.

Caroline Sheldon Literary Agency for 'Keep Your Airplanes Away From Our Islands' 1995,
'Nobody Rides The Unicorn' 1995, 'Nothingmas Day'; 'Rat-It-Up', 'Not A Very Cheerful Song
I'm Afraid', 'Fruit Jokes', 'School Dinners' from All My Own Stuff published by Simon &
Schuster Young Books 1991; 'Yes' from Ten Banana More published by Simon & Schuster
Young Books 1994.

Rogers Coleridge and White Ltd for 'Dear Mum', 'Invisible Dog', 'Playing Football With
The Dog', 'Grumbly Moon', 'You Can't Be That' and 'The Pet Wig' from Thawing Frozen Frogs
© Brian Patten 1990 first published by Viking; 'Uncle Ben From Number One' and
'The Pet Habit' from The Utter Nutters © Brian Patten 1994 first published by Viking;
'Guess What Dad Does', 'Gust Becos I Cud Not Spel', 'Burying The Dog In The Garden'
from Gargling With Jelly © Brian Patten 1985 first published by Viking Children's Books;
'My Dancing Granny' © Brian Patten 1995.

A selected list of poetry books available from Macmillan

The prices shown below are correct at the time of going to press. However, Macmillan Publishers reserve the right to show new retail prices on covers which may differ from those previously advertised.

One of Your Legs is Both the Same   0 330 32704 6
   Henri, Jones, Rosen, Wright & McNaughton   £3.99

Another Day on Your Foot and I Would Have Died   0 330 34048 4
   Agard, Cope, McGough, Mitchell & Patten   £3.99

We Couldn't Provide Fish Thumbs   0 330 35236 9
   Berry, Nicholls, Nichols, Scannell & Sweeney   £3.99

Cockcrow to Starlight   0 330 34265 7
   Edited by Rumer Godden   £4.99

Selected Poems for Children   0 330 35404 3
   Charles Causley   £5.99

A Spell of Words   0 330 35422 1
   Elizabeth Jennings   £4.99

Glitter When You Jump   0 330 34104 9
   Edited by Fiona Waters   £3.99

All Macmillan titles can be ordered at your local bookshop or are available by post from:

**Book Service by Post
PO Box 29, Douglas, Isle of Man IM99 1BQ**

Credit cards accepted. For details:
Telephone: 01624 675137
Fax: 01624 670923
E-mail: bookshop@enterprise.net

Free postage and packing in the UK.
Overseas customers: add £1 per book (paperback)
and £3 per book (hardback).